Just be yourself!

- time *just for you* **to be <u>yourself</u> -**
before your God

<u>By</u>   <u>Annette Baines</u>

Annette Baines

All scripture references are taken from Holy Bible, New International Version 1998.

Thanks.. I would like to thank everyone who has given permission to include material in this book. I wanted to trace, acknowledge and seek permission for inclusion of material of jokes and quotations and I apologise for any omissions. This is my first book and I would not wish to offend anyone. Please feel free to contact me if you wish.

Published and Printed by
Leiston Press Ltd
Masterlord Industrial Estate
Leiston
Suffolk
IP16 4JD
Telephone Number: 01728 833003
Email: glenn@leistonpress.com
Web: www.leistonpress.com

ISBN 978-1-911311-21-8

DEDICATION

I dedicate this book to our daughter Nicola who was the inspiration for writing this book.

Nicola is a good wife, a loving mother and a wonderful person.

THANKS

My grateful thanks go to my wonderful husband David and son Martin who have been living in the same house with me whilst I wrote this. How patient is that!! Thanks go to David for proof reading and making suggestions and also to Martin for technical advice, computer help and encouragement! I must mention Matt too (our son-in-law). I prayed for a Christian husband for our Nicola and here you are!! I didn't know you then but God did!!

Thanks to Mary, Ann, Veronica, Avril, Shannon, Sylvia, Jenny and Steve, and Mel. Your encouragement and prayers are much appreciated as always!!

I want to say a big THANK YOU to Gill and Skippy Gifford of Cutting Edge Ministries for their constant encouragement and prayer for my husband, my family and myself. Their faithful ministry of encouragement to all Christians everywhere to live at their fullest potential for God has been awesome.

Contents page

Chapter		page

1. You are Precious to God!

You are the apple of His eye, you are His beloved child and He delights in you.

God can provide all the answers to your questions of '**how can I get through this busy day**?' You can launch yourself into the day and work things out in your own strength or you can surrender your day into God's hands.

God wants to take your burdens from you but *won't* do so *without your permission.* I myself learnt late that I needed to name and give God my burdens each day. God has our best interests at heart and hears every prayer.

You can confide all your anxieties to Him. You can put yourself and your family in prayer at the foot of the cross. He can help, support and encourage you *in any situation.* He can take your burdens and can answer prayers powerfully as only He has *the total picture*; only He knows everything that has gone before. You won't regret spending time with God.

God delights in you and loves to spend time with you!

LOOKING AT YOUR CHILD

My prayer for you is that, as you read this book, you will realise how precious **you are** to God. When you look at your child with love and pride, remember that this is how God looks at you. When your child disappoints you, remember that sometimes maybe God is disappointed with us BUT his love is unconditional and never-ending. He still looks at you with love and approval.

God is the best role model for parenthood that there is and ever will be. When reading the Bible, we can see this. There is **nothing** that cannot be confided to Him. He is there for us all 24/7. All we have to do is turn to Him, confess and want to be rid of (repent of) any sin and ask for change. Our sin is taken away and He then has our permission to help us and make changes that we want.

GOD LOVES YOU IN A WAY NO ONE ELSE CAN..

You are the apple of his eye. No matter what the world has thrown at you; he sees real potential in you. You don't have to do anything to earn his approval and love – it is there *always.* He is your Father and delights in you. He is interested in you and all you do. You are precious to God.

FRIENDSHIP

I talk to God as my friend because He is my heavenly Father and He cares about me deeply. I am **not** irreverent but I am just myself. I have prayed to him in every place you could think of! I have entreated, praised, thanked and shouted at God. I have ALWAYS been myself. What's the point of being otherwise? He knows everything about me anyway!!

I hope you will find the prayers here helpful and use or adapt them as you feel.

I suggest that, if you are busy, just read the verses of scripture. These are your food and will build your relationship with God.

WHY INCLUDE THE JOKES?

Laughter is a joy and a gift from God. The jokes make us realise that we all experience similar problems and difficulties in parenthood and marriage and we are not perfect. We can laugh at our situations; we can know that **'we do what we can**

do' and **'do our best'** and we can know with certainty that God looks at us laughing with approval and love.

I hope you enjoy this book, have fun and happiness as a parent and remember that failure can also be a stepping stone to success!!

Little girl to friend, 'I'm never having a baby.'

'Why?' asked the other girl.

'Well, they take 9 months to download!' (anon)

Kitchen mutterings!! Have you heard any of this before?
- Take us as we come or not at all!
- If I had a posh kitchen, I wouldn't cook in it!
- Don't moan about this kitchen – loads of people have eaten my meals and I haven't caused food poisoning yet!
- WHY can't you use a board when making sarnies? Or clean up after you? I know they're only crumbs but they belong in the bin – not my worktop!
- Please wash the dirty dishes in the oven.They are our breakfast pots. Auntie Meg came so we did a massive tidy!!
- Our kitchen doesn't always look like this, you know!! Most of the time it's FAR worse!
- A balanced diet is a cup cake in each hand!
- Don't watch me while I cook or I'll burn the tea.

- Yes I KNOW too much coffee makes me irritable so just be quiet and read the paper!!
- I'd rather not eat that Mum – it's too healthy.
- Yes, I know that sweet things are bad for the teeth Mum but I've had a really busy day!
- Yes I know it's my job to take the rubbish out and I haven't bothered all week but I do have homework three times a week now you know!
- Yes, I noticed you did a huge supermarket shop, but I couldn't find anything decent to eat so I ordered a takeaway.
- You've just GOT to have bad days so when you get good ones you really appreciate them!!
- I KNOW we don't use all the fancy kitchen gadgets but people who come THINK we do so it's worth having them!
- This is a self-cleaning kitchen. Clean up after yourself (or else…!!)
- If you just accept me as I am you are welcome to visit ANYTIME.

2.   God Will Get You Through!

I *worked outside* the home while my children were small; I also had times when I **didn't** work and was *at home* with my children; there were times I *worked at home* and **also** was at home with my children.

Some of my complaints when at <u>work</u> were that I –

never had enough energy;

never had time for a quiet time with God;

could never catch up with the housework;

worried about people dropping in as our house was not 'up to scratch';

didn't see my friends as often as I liked;

I was worried about childcare arrangements;

I worried that I should be doing more with my children;

I had no time for myself.

My complaints <u>as a homemaker</u> were not much different. I -

never had enough energy;

never had time for a quiet time with God;

could never catch up with the housework;

worried about people dropping in as home was often in chaos;

didn't see my friends as often as I liked;

I worried that I should be doing more with my children;

I had no time for myself.

When I talk to young mums, a lot of their issues are the same. I make them laugh at some of the things I share but it also takes pressure off them when I chat. ***<u>Pressure is what the world gives us as we try to conform to other people's expectations</u>***. When you realise that others go through the same things it helps! When someone confesses their failures or triumphs, it helps! So why can't we just be ourselves?

Have you ever heard the phrases 'good enough' or 'doing what I can do' or 'doing my best'? When you listen to someone who has 'been there', you get things into perspective and you relax. **_You can only do what you can do_**. After all, motherhood should be a joy and you should be fun to be with – not like me, as I constantly put burdens upon myself that I now believe God didn't want me to bear.

If I had put my relationship with God *FIRST* then I would have enjoyed my motherhood more. I wish I had just been myself.

Just be yourself. God loves you!

Do you agree? When you have bad days it's awful, *but* it makes you appreciate the good days all the more!!

3. Rise and Shine

Psalm 5 verse 3

"In the morning, O Lord, you hear my voice; in the morning, I lay my requests before you and wait in expectation."

I love this scripture. I realise that as I pray, God can distinguish my voice as being me and me alone. He knows ME intimately and responds to ME. As my husband prays, God recognises his voice as being HIM and HIM alone. He knows HIM intimately and responds to HIM. It is the same for all of us; God has no favourites.

Since we know, then, that each of us is different and special and loved by God, then we can have confidence in bringing all of our concerns, worries and troubles to Him.

We can all lay our requests before Him, knowing that He responds to us intimately.

My husband is not a morning person – sometimes he still seems fast asleep when we pray. We have to persevere because it draws us closer together. Praying together is special for us. Ecclesiastes 4 verse 12 says....'**a cord of three strands is not quickly broken**.' There is power and an increase of love when we pray with our husbands. God ordained for a man and a woman to be together and so he enjoys being with us and blesses us. He knows all we go through.

Is your husband a non-Christian? God hears your faithful prayers and will bless you. In the morning, as the Psalmist says, He hears your voice. He knows all you go through. He will come close to you if you come close to Him.

<u>**Lord,** thank you! I am special to you! In the morning, I want to praise and thank you as well as ask you to help. Come into my heart and let me feel you close to me all day long. Thanks for being a loving heavenly father.</u> **Amen.**

Psalm 40 verse 4

"Blessed is the man who makes the Lord his trust."

Psalm 92 verses 1 and 2

"It is good to praise the Lord

And make music to your name, O Most High,

To proclaim your love in the morning

And your faithfulness at night."

Psalm 121 verses 1 and 2

I lift up my eyes to the hills –

Where does my help come from?

My help comes from the Lord,

The maker of heaven and earth.

ACTS – I use this acronym to jog my memory sometimes in my prayer time.

You might find it helpful too in your prayer time.

A   adoration – tell God what you think of Him,

C   confession – confess your sins

T   thanks – for answered prayers, provision, protection and for loving you!

S   supplication – give Him your burdens (what is on your heart – anxieties, problems etc.).

Ask for help.

4.   A Home

Home is where you put in your culture and your morals.

(A Traveller)

Home is not a place; it is a sense of belonging.

(An immigrant)

If we think about phrases like 'feel at home' or 'home from home' or 'make yourself at home' we realise that home is intended to be a place where people feel secure and relaxed. They can be themselves at home – no pretence. This is why people say they 'long to get home' and talk about 'home sweet home'. They can just be or feel or look at home because the word home signifies a safe place; a happy place where you and your family live and are cared for. Home seems to be a place where you belong.

If home for someone is *not* a safe place then the word home can cause anxiety. If you hate the idea of 'home' or 'family' then you cringe when people use these words affectionately. You may not know how to create a home. The Traveller (above) had many homes and schools in her life but the feeling of home for her was that of belonging to her family and to her extended traveller family.

I was speaking to someone who told me she didn't understand what home is about – in all weathers she was sent out to play and as soon as she was on the 'dole' as a youngster was kicked out of her home to fend for herself as a young teenager.

She never sees her father now and has only just got in touch with her mother but does not trust her mother at all. The only feeling of belonging she gets is from supporting a sports' team; otherwise, she is completely self sufficient.

What does home mean to you? Is there anything from your own childhood that is preventing you from creating a home? Do you hate the word 'family' or does it cause you stress because you don't know what it really means?

Be aware that, when we feel anxious about something, we can over-compensate which can cause problems in the future. The only way is to pray and ask for help.

Heavenly Father, I belong to you.

I have difficulties with memories of my childhood and this is affecting my relationships and my creation of a home. I give these memories to you _____
and ask that you help me to come to terms with

_____

Please help me. I want to know how to make a home and not go overboard trying to do too much. I really need your wisdom each day Lord God and I ask that you guide my thinking about motherhood and family.

Or ..

<u>My Father God</u>. I belong to you.

Today is a new day. Help me walk with you and show me how to create a safe, welcoming, happy home where everyone's needs are met. I want my home to be a special place where people long to return to.

Show me the meaning of the words 'home' and 'family' and help me to be the person you created me to be. Guide my thinking about my marriage and parenthood. **Amen.**

5. Idols

Psalm 135 verses 15-18 *"The idols of the nation are silver and gold, made by the hands of men. They have mouths but cannot speak, eyes, but they cannot see; they have ears but cannot hear nor is there breath in their mouths. Those who make them will be like them, and so will all who trust in them."*

Do you agree that you should never worship an idol made out of wood or clay? BUT should you worship your husband? Or your children? Or home? Or pop stars?

An idol is anything that takes the place of God, so if you idolise ANYTHING or ANYONE.. your husband, your children, your work, football, your car, your home – anything – you will not see God the way He truly is. You will hear the Word but not fully understand it. You will see other Christians draw near to God but you may feel that *you* can't hear God. You might wonder why others seem close to God and you don't. You might even feel detached or cold towards God.

If you think about it, you are putting things or people in God's true place. They are the brick wall to your relationship with God. It's not that you shouldn't love your family or work or car or home or football, but it's important to put God first. You'll have a relationship with Him that will make you feel blessed and secure. What happens then is that you are blessed in your marriage, your family, your home and all that matters to you.

Father God,

I want to know you and have a daily relationship with you. I realise that I might have made a barrier between myself and you by making you insignificant when compared to all that I care about. You see and know all of this. You tell me in the Word that you are a jealous God. Help me to give you the right place in my life so that all will go well with me. Open the eyes of my heart so that I can see you as you truly are.

Father God, I confess that I do idolise………………….
…………………… I repent.

Please forgive me for this. Show me how to put you first as all of my blessings come from you. Let me remember this all the days of my life.

Deuteronomy 32 verse 16

"They made him jealous with their foreign gods and angered him with their detestable idols."

Proverbs 14 verse 12

"There is a way that seems right to man but in the end it leads to death."

Isaiah 44 verse 9

"All who make idols are nothing,

And the things they treasure are worthless."

1 John 5 verse 21

"My children, keep yourselves from idols."

6.   Being a Home Maker!

Colossians 3 verse 23

"Whatever you do, work at it with all your heart, as working for the Lord, not for men."

If you have decided not to work whilst bringing up your children you are able to have time to encourage and teach them about the Lord. I had periods of time when I worked and then there were times when I did not. I found the time at home with my children to be extremely isolating even though I loved them very much. The solution for me was to attend a women's group with a crèche where I could try crafts, listen to talks, play sport and talk to other women. It was a tremendous encouragement to me and I know other women felt the same. Whether you work or not God will bless you when you spend time with your children but you also need time for yourself.

I found that I was a far better mother when I had an occasional break from my children. My friendships were important to me.

I was then able to concentrate on my family. We are taught that whatever we do we should do as if we were working for God. There is no higher calling for a woman than to teach her children all about the love of God and encourage them to have a personal relationship with Him.

How can we teach our children about God?

By reading the Bible aloud each day, singing worship songs, by playing age appropriate DVDs, CDs of Bible stories. Encourage the children to explore the story e.g. you can make little baskets with shredded wheat crackle cakes with marzipan baby Moses inside. You can replay the story of David and Goliath by dressing up, making a paper bag with rubbers inside to represent the stones. Goliath could be drawn on wallpaper and stuck on an outside wall so 'David' could throw the 'stones' at him.

If your children are having behavioural difficulties you can use the Bible stories for moral teaching ....caring for one another (Moses, psalms, proverbs, Good Samaritan), problems with siblings (Joseph, Jacob and Esau)...friendship (David and Jonathan).. loyalty (Ruth)...bravery (Esther) ...prayer (Hannah)......bullying (David and Goliath). Encourage your children to talk to you about the stories they read and help them to revisit them and recap so that they remember them.

Finish the stories with a prayer – e.g. – *Father God, help me not to be worried or frightened by bullies. Help me to say the name of Jesus in my head whenever I am scared. Look after me and keep me safe at all times. Show me what to say when…….   Show me what to do when ……..'*

Psalm 4 verse 8

"I will lie down and sleep in peace, for you alone, O Lord, make me dwell in safety."

7. Getting Close to God

Hebrews 4 verse 12

"For the word of God is living and active.

Sharper than any double-edged sword."

If you are a Christian, people tell you that you need to be reading the Bible every day. You might say why bother? You get enough Bible verses in Church or remember the Bible from Sunday school or youth group.

We are taught *people's views* of the Bible in Church. Definitely, they quote the Bible but it is the way they interpret it that can be wrong or dangerous. If you are not reading your Bible and someone has wrong teaching then you may ***not*** be able to discern that it ***is*** wrong. If you are communicating with God daily in prayer and praise and reading the Word and one day your preacher says anything wrong you will feel unease in your spirit if it's wrong so it is then worthwhile praying about it.

Sometimes in a Meeting, I ask God to guard my Spirit and to accept only what He wants me to learn and to discern truth at all times.

There is no substitute for truth. There is no substitute for your own relationship with God. Reading the Word is difficult when you feel too tired to think but reading the Bible will have an impact on your life and will give you deep joy if you persevere. It is your daily food to help you everyday.

I found reading the Bible hard because I read very fast; can quickly skim read to get the 'gist' and I love reading. ***Reading the Bible without meditating on it is like trying to eat without swallowing (anonymous***).

How true! I couldn't remember it!

My prayer partners were able to quote the Bible and use the Bible verses to declare over any situation we were praying for. I asked God to help me do the same and I do so love the Bible now. I meditate on it and I can say that it gives me deep joy.

Father God,

I don't want to be taught any lies about you. I can trust my Church Leaders but help me to remember that you are God and they are only human. Help me to be faithful to you the way that you are faithful to me.

Help me to have a daily relationship with you and help me to ENJOY reading the Word and meditating on what you are saying to me personally through the Word. Never allow me or my family to be deceived by any wrong teaching in a Church, through friendship, on TV, on the internet, in a book or in any Meeting. ***I want to be close to you every day God.***

Words of Encouragement

Deuteronomy 11 verse 18

"Fix these words of mine in your hearts and minds….."

Psalm 12 verse 6

"And the words of the Lord are flawless, like silver refined in a furnace of clay, purified seven times."

2 Corinthians 2 verse 17

"..we do not peddle the word of God for profit. On the contrary, in Christ we speak before God with sincerity, like men sent from God."

Jokes!

A Joke Backfires -

A Preacher who found humour difficult attended a conference to help encourage and better equip clergy in their ministry. He wanted to teach people about the Bible using everyday illustrations so paid real attention to this man who declared, 'the best years of my life were spent in the arms of a woman who was not my wife!' Everyone was shocked but he ended, 'and that woman was my mother!' People laughed and listened attentively.

The preacher decided to use the same joke in his own church. He tried to rehearse the joke but couldn't quite remember. He spoke loudly into the microphone. 'The greatest years of my life were spent in the arms of another woman who was not my wife!' The congregation gasped. He tried desperately to remember the punch line……………

'And I can't remember who she was!' (anon.)

A boy watched his Dad, a pastor, write his sermon.

'How do you know what to say?' he asked

'Why – God tells me,' said Dad.

'Oh! Why do you keep crossing things out?' he asked.

Unlock the mysteries of God. Jesus is the key. God is bigger than any Church.

8. Surrendering Your Parenthood to God

Luke chapter 7 verse 7

"She gave birth to her firstborn, a son. She wrapped him in cloths and placed him in a manger, because there was no room for them at the inn."

When you hold your new baby in your arms, there are overwhelming feelings. What did **YOU** think about when you held your child? When we had our first child – a daughter – I felt completely blessed by the Lord. We had tried to have children for so long and here she was – our little daughter. It was like a bombshell had exploded in our quiet cottage. She was lively, funny, special, full of energy! We had so many hopes and dreams for her.

When we held our second child – a boy – the same feelings were there. Our son was lively, funny, special and full of energy. We were now doubly blessed. Two lovely children. Two lovely children given to us by God to love and care for.

What do you think Mary thought as she held her special baby? Do you think she was content to place her precious child wrapped in cloths in a dusty, prickly food manger trough? What thoughts were in her head about her special son? Did she have hopes and dreams?

I would imagine that she would talk to God about her child at the beginning and throughout his life. After all, when the Angel Gabriel visited Mary to tell her she would be Jesus' mother, despite being disturbed by the news, she accepted God's will for her life. **She *surrendered* to *God's will for her parenthood*** even though it would not be her preferred way of starting married life. Mary also praised God mightily when she visited her cousin Elizabeth which shows an understanding and love of God. Elizabeth realised that Mary put her trust in God – Luke 1 verse 45 **"blessed is she who has believed that what the Lord has said to her will be accomplished.'** We also have to trust our children to God.

Have you surrendered your parenthood to God?

I didn't do that because I was a fairly new Christian and didn't know how. I could not have done anymore for my children than I did and I had hopes and dreams. I did my absolute best. God told me I was not a failure. I had wonderful parents who had modelled good parenthood. However, I *know* that, if I had surrendered my parenthood to God I would have been a more successful, relaxed parent.

Father God,

I would like to trust you as Mary did. Parenthood is unknown. Each child is different and only you truly understand the needs of each child. I surrender my child into your hands Father God.

I surrender my parenthood into your hands Father God and ask for your Holy Spirit to guide me. I ask that you help me at all times. If I fail in any way, help me to quickly confess this to you and to forgive myself and move on and learn from my mistakes. Help me to be the loving parent that you are, Father God. **Amen**.

Luke 1 verse 46

"And Mary said: My soul glorifies the Lord and my spirit rejoices in God my Saviour."

9. The Ballad of a New Baby!

by *Annette Baines*

A baby comes into the house

To make your life complete.

A few short hours in the house

And you're dropping on your feet!

Your baby cries around the clock,

It needs you all the time.

You feed and wash and clean and yawn

And wonder - WHERE – goes time?

Smell the baby's silky skin

And touch the downy hair.

Listen to the gurgly talk

And watch an infant stare!

Your baby knows you are nearby

And follows you by sound.

Your every movement gives such peace;

Sleep creeps on face, so round.

Your baby lights up every day

With gorgeous baby smiles.

You have a special loving bond

And laughter all the while.

Your child – SO precious to our God,

The apple of His eye.

YOU are SO precious to our God,

The apple of His eye.

Each baby is a gift from God

To make your life complete.

God loves you ALL so very much

In Him ALL are complete.

10. Liking Your Child and Trusting God

Malachi chapter 4 v 6

"He will turn the hearts of the fathers to their children, and the hearts of the children to their fathers.."

In Charles Dickens 'Dombey and Son' (chapter 4) two ladies were bewailing the fact that the father of baby Florence could not be close to his daughter. This is because 'Florence will never, never, never be a Dombey..' In other words, Florence favoured her mother and these good ladies could see that her father was not going to be close to Florence because of this.

What happens when a baby is born? Am I right in saying that we all have hopes, dreams and fears for their future? What do we do when we are musical and our child is not? Or we love art and our child hates it? What if there has been a divorce and the child we have reminds us of its absent parent (unfavourably) at every twist and turn?

I imagine that there have been times in my life when I have disappointed God, making bad choices and being wilful or stubborn. However, God was there at the beginning of my life and knows everything about me. He looks on what I have done and it may sorrow Him but He also looks to what I can become. He accepts and loves me as I am, warts and all. His love is *faithful, unconditional and unending.* I am the apple of His eye, I am His precious child, ***just as you are, just as all of us are.*** It is difficult to love someone who irritates you or you feel you have no connection with. It might just be your past or post natal depression; it could be that your idea of parenthood is completely opposite to what you have got. No one really understands family relationships but you can rely on God. He has the total picture. He can deliver, rescue, mend, restore and call into being that which is not. *This child has been given to you by God for a purpose. It is part of **your ministry to Him** that you bring up this child in your home.* Rejection is unthinkable. It kills self-esteem and self-respect. God is waiting to partner with you if you will ask Him. He can change hearts and transform families.

Father God,

I confess that I do not love my child the way I should. I feel_____because_____

_____

Please will you heal any memories of

_____

Please will you give me your love for this child at all times. Help me to see my child the way you do. By the authority you have given me in Jesus' name, I stand against the wiles of the devil and I resist rebellion, stubbornness and disrespect from me and to me by my child. Help me to remember that I am my child's role model.

How I am with my child will be how my child will be to me.

I pray that this relationship will not be subject to destruction now or in the future.

Soften our hearts towards each other please.

Help us daily to see each other the way you do and help us to love each other the way you do. Amen

11. Our Words

Proverbs 16 verse 32

"Better a patient man than a warrior, A man who controls his temper than one who takes a city."

Don't you think children are amazing? They can't remember where their book bags are but they always remember the row you had with your husband at breakfast.

Mornings are often fraught. Time is like sand; it slips through the fingers. A woman has a fantastic ability for feeding the cat then feeding the family whilst ironing a school shirt and completing a form for school that just HAS to be in today. Sometimes though it's all too much and temper kicks in. I've always been a feisty person so I remember it well!

Children are like sponges. The way we are with our husbands is absorbed into their memories. When Dad swears after hammering his finger by mistake, it gets absorbed. When Grandma can't find her false teeth, this episode is absorbed. Even when we think they are playing quietly and not taking anything in, what we are saying is being absorbed. I was really **red-faced** when I went to collect my daughter and her best buddy from Nursery one day. We had taken them to a friend's house the week before for a prayer meeting. They were only three but we were amazed that they played together quietly whilst we had a time of prayer. Unfortunately, they had absorbed what we had said and it was repeated whilst they played together in the sandpit. Apparently, all of the Nursery staff were convulsed with laughter. I don't **quite** know what was said even now!

If we are loving towards our husbands, they absorb it. If we say 'sorry' to our husbands, our children and anyone else (even the cat!) this gets absorbed. If we read our Bibles, this gets absorbed. I was sitting quietly with my tiny grandson one day and he suddenly said,' Grandma, you love God and you love Jesus.' I was amazed but told him he was right.

Do you spend time with your children reading Bible stories, praying together and living the Christian life together?

Some Christians believe they should let their children make up their own minds about God. This is true but, also, someone pointed out that you protect your children by teaching them how to be safe on the roads. Therefore, you can keep them safe by teaching them all that you know about God and Jesus without being pushy or overbearing. If you 'walk the walk' of faith, they will want this for themselves.

If you teach them all that they need to know about the Christian faith *at the very least* this will be good moral teaching and *at the very most* it will lead them to salvation.

Father,

Please will you partner with me in bringing up my beloved child(ren). I need your wisdom, your words and your help to witness in a loving but powerful way. Protect our family and help us to bear with one another.

Increase our faith daily and help us all to see you and your son Jesus Christ the way you truly are. Amen.

Colossians 3 verse 13   Bear with one another and forgive whatever grievances you may have against one other. Forgive as the Lord forgave

12. Protecting Your Children

Proverbs 22 verse 6

"Train a child in the way he should go, and when he is old he will not turn from it."

If you are a parent who drowns her sorrows or eases stress in alcohol or overeating or drugs then it is likely that your addictive behaviour will affect your children. If you are impatient, angry, abusive or discouraging then it is likely that your children will be too. This is not condemning; it is the truth. My children are grown now but I can see the way that we have lived has had an effect on their lives. I used sugary foods to give me an 'oomph' when I was so weary and I have noticed our children doing the same. When tired, I was snappy and I have noticed even the same words used by our children when they are too.

My dictionary defined training as, 'to draw on; to instruct and discipline; to cause to grow in the desired manner.' I have never been the totally perfect mother but I have demonstrated that my faith is real, that my faith has been constant and consistent (and has even grown!) and that I have a daily relationship with God.

I did not always ask the Holy Spirit to guide me in bringing up our children. I noticed that, when I worked in my own strength, gritting my teeth, screwing up my courage to keep going, I *failed*. When I tried to be the perfect parent, *I failed*. When I acknowledged my weaknesses before God and called out for help, then *I succeeded*. I certainly tried to make my children see that God loved them no matter what. I asked my children to forgive me when I was snappy and I now have a scar on my face when I broke out in spots because of my sugar addiction. Most of all, I learned that I am not perfect and that I need to forgive myself too.

Heavenly Father,

Children are precious and I don't want to be a bad parent. Help me to be the parent you created me to be. You allow me to fail sometimes and I need to treat this as a learning curve rather than condemnation and to forgive myself and move on.

Fill me with your Holy Spirit to guide me through every day. Give me your wisdom, kindness and love for my children. Help me to always see the good in them and love them the way they need to be loved. Help me to talk to you and give you my concerns and requests for them at every twist and turn of their lives. Enable me to instruct and discipline my children in a godly manner. You see all that I do. Guide me Lord.

Please grow a deep love for you and your ways within my children. Amen.

** When you are at the end of your tether and feel weak, tearful and fed up, you will find God is waiting to give you a God hug Ask him to show you how much He loves you and tell Him how you feel. **

13. Train a Child

Proverbs 22 verse 6

"Train a child in the way he should go, and when he is old he will not turn from it."

Let me be nosy. What do you have in your home? TV? Computer? DVD? CDs? Books? How many of them are Christian DVDs or books?

When I was a young Mum, I was challenged by a preacher one morning. He asked us to do a mental check and think – how many Christian books did we have for our children? I love books and tried hard to nurture a love of reading in our children but had to confess that the non-christian books **outnumbered** the Christian. He then challenged us further. What proportion of our everyday life is spent sharing about our love of God and Jesus to our children? Again, I fell short. The preacher pointed out that we have to keep a balance - it's hard for our children not to know about suitable worldly literature and DVDs and TV programmes because they need to fit in with school friends; they need to be part of the world. However, the emphasis should be on Christian teaching because it is their food. **At the very least it teaches moral truths but at the very most it leads to faith in God.** We think about evangelising our neighbours and friends but teaching our children is even more important. ***They are the future***. They are a gift from God. Also, it's easier to think of fun ways of sharing our faith because we know the characters of our children and what appeals to them.

How can we do this?

- ✓ Visit a Christian bookshop and browse Sunday school teaching resources for ideas or look in charity shops for bible craft resources.
- ✓ Buy age-appropriate, appealing Bibles for your children and encourage them to read them every day with you. At holiday times, let them select verses to illustrate and then give these away to Christian friends as birthday/christmas cards, or photocopy for calendars.
- ✓ Find out about foods in Bible times and use some to cook with the children.
- ✓ At problem times e.g. friendship or family breakups, bullying etc. select Bible stories which link in (e.g. the breakdown of family relationships with Joseph and subsequent reconciliation, or the bullying of Goliath - and David calling on God's power to deal with this).
- ✓ Have a family time in the evening. We used to have a candle lamp in the evening which was lit and then we had a time of sharing and prayers. It was a time when I tried to show the children how much I loved them and a time of security and peace. A calm exit to bed!!
- ✓ Don't read *any* non-christian books just before bed. Read them early on.
- ✓ An appealing children's Bible, a rusk or biscuit and milk helped me to settle them!
  Peace!

Father, You have given us your sense of fun. Help us to have fun together. Be in all of the family times where we share about you and let us all, adults and children, grow in the knowledge and love of you and of each other. Amen

Proverbs 23 verse 15

"My son if your heart is wise then my heart will be glad. "

(or we might say My daughter!!)

14. Let Go and Let God!

Psalm 145 verse 14

"The Lord upholds all those who fall and lifts up all who are bowed down."

Tiredness is a killer!! It can wreck your patience, your peace and your parenthood.

I travelled 130 miles to support my elderly Mum once or twice a month. I worked full time in my husband's business, often putting the children to bed and then working till midnight. I did some temporary jobs as well. With 2 very lively children, I felt I had to be a perfect mother and tried to do my very best for them. We went out nearly every day and I played with them at home, often too tired to talk to my husband when he came in. After awhile, I realised I was on a treadmill of my own making. I'd tried to do so much in my own strength and to be honest I failed!! I surrendered all to God and He provided a support system. God displayed His loving parenthood to me as he showed me the way forward and took the strain. He also showed me how I had neglected my husband. I learnt that I can do nothing, *but God can do everything when I ask for help.*

Do you ever struggle with living? Do you want to live a victorious life? *Take it from me who failed.* You can't be successful entirely in your own strength. <u>Let go and let God.</u> Surrender all your concerns in prayer. I've never regretted it.

Dear Father God, You are so good to those who put their trust in you. You know we're weak and anxious. Before we speak, you already know the problems and there is no situation that you cannot help us with.

Father, I need your wisdom, your strength, your words, your love, your peace. Help me to partner in parenthood with you. Help me to surrender all my concerns to you and not to charge on in my own strength. You are amazing God!

Please carry me when I am exhausted or upset and help me to demonstrate your love to my family always. Amen

Psalm 139 verse 4

"Before a word is on my tongue you know it completely O Lord."

Lamentations 3 verse 25 *"The Lord is good to those whose hope is in him, to the one who seeks him."*

Lamentations 3 verse 22

"Because of the Lord's great love we are not consumed, for his compassions never fail."

Psalm 126 verse 5

"Those who sow in tears will reap in songs of joy."

Learning to let go and let God

My husband and I needed to replace our car and we discussed for weeks which one was suitable.

My husband was desperate for a car which drove like a sports car but accepted that he probably couldn't have the one he wanted as we had two small children. However, he did not want a 'run of the mill' car and had strong views on this. I was *adamant* that we needed a sensible family car with a big boot. Discussions dragged on for weeks and then went into arguments as frustration hit us both.

Eventually, we sat down and asked God to forgive us for being unloving and we repented. We then told God what we wanted. Within a short time, my husband was prompted to look at a car he had never even thought about. It was ideal – ample boot space and drove like a sports car!

We loved this car so much we bought another second-hand one for me! Isn't God good!!

Ecclesiastes 4 v 12

"A cord of three strands is not quickly broken."

Laugh at your arguments – everyone else does!! (anonymous)

Jon discovered that women regularly use 30,000 words but men use only 15,000.

Jon had long held the conviction that his wife talked too much so was keen to point this out to her.

His wife listened and then thought for awhile.

'It's because we have to repeat everything we say.'

'What?' asked Jon.

15. Count Your Blessings!

Psalm 54 verse 4

"Surely God is my help; the Lord is the one who sustains me."

When you're struggling with lack of money, smelly socks, sick on duvets and no time or money for yourself, it's easy to think you have no blessings! Tiredness can make you look on the black side of life.

What can you do?

- Meet up with other Christian women.
- Ask God to give you energy and wisdom.
- Make space for **you** each day – a bubblebath, a walk, a book, a jigsaw, sewing.
- Share childcare prayerfully. Trusted friends can help you today; you look after their children tomorrow.
- Do what my friend does. When tired, put all your washing up in the oven to wash tomorrow (don't forget to write yourself a note!).
- Prepare evening meal in the morning when you have more energy.
- Have a list of easy 'bad day'/rainy day activities to do with the children.

PRAYER

My Father God, I'm struggling
with_____

Please can you help me order my day so I'm not exhausted every night. I want to be a good wife and mum, but please help me to make time for myself and not to feel guilty for anything which has not been achieved. Help me to give thanks for -

- Your love for me
- My family
- My friends
- My belongings that you have given me
- Your provision

1 Chronicles 16 verse 11

"Look to the Lord and his strength; seek his face always."

1 Thessalonians chapter 5 verse 16

"Be joyful always; pray continually; give thanks in all circumstances, for this is God's will for you in Christ Jesus."

Philippians 4 verse 6

"Do not be anxious about anything but in all things, by prayer and petition with thanksgiving, present your requests to God."

<u>Examples of easy/bad day activities with children</u>

TODDLERS *Go outside and blow bubbles

*If you are busy give your toddler a bowl of water, bubbles and some unbreakable things to 'wash' (this will get on the floor so a mop would be handy or you could put large bath towels down).

*Your child can sort out a pile of carrots, onions, swede etc. for you to peel for tea.

<u>Wash child's hands thoroughly afterwards</u>.

* Give your child a special safety child knife or a round ended knife and with your constant support and help (you need to

press as they won't have finger strength) show them how to chop up a peeled potato and then put it with a 'plop' into water in the pan.

*bring home a cardboard box and let them play with it.

* make a den with a cloth draped over a table. Allow child to use old curtains or cloths and cushions to put in the den. This keeps them quiet for *ages* but you will find all sorts of things taken underneath!

*fuzzy felts are good to calm toddlers.

* play dough can absorb youngsters (you can buy pots to keep for rainy days).

*Give child clean paintbrushes and a bucket of clean water and they can 'paint' the outside wall or shed on a sunny day.

* Allow them to play with torches on a dark Winter's day.

* Kick the leaves in Autumn. Collect some leaves, take home and dip in paint and print on paper (not MUCH mess if you put newspaper down).

*If you have any cooked warm **(not hot)** pasta/rice leftover put it in a bowl for your child to play with. Leftover jelly is good for them to play with also. It may be messy but keeps children absorbed for ages.

OLDER CHILDREN

*Play clay, play dough or salt dough are useful. You can buy or make.

*Sort a button box by colour and shape and put sets of buttons in small freezer bags.

*On a rainy day go to a museum or art gallery. Take children home and give them paints or dough to make their own masterpieces!

*Quick on the draw Bible game. Each person has a closed Bible. Count down from 5-1, name a book and then the first person to find the book in the Bible is the winner. Reward with raisins or counters. Person with most could choose an activity for the next day (best for you to give a choice of say four activities that you could cope with before you start the game!!).

* Select suitable Bible verses for cards and use materials to illustrate cards for family birthdays or calendars.

*Make Appreciation Cards or large Bookmarks. Child has to think of one good thing to say about the recipient e.g. Bookmark for Auntie Alice – 'You are great Auntie! I appreciate you because you take me to the cinema. Thanks!... 'Child can illustrate it.

* Provide cardboard box, puppets and ideas for a play e.g. Pinocchio. Children make up a play and make a theatre from cardboard box (you might have to help with cutting). Children can perform to family. They could also make sweets for their guests (look at child's cookery books for non cooked sweets).

*Child draws favourite character, colours and then cuts out. They can then be stuck onto pencils or straws and used as puppets.

16. God wants to bless you on Sundays!

Exodus 20 verse 8

"Remember the Sabbath day by keeping it holy."

Tiredness can make us angry or depressed. 'Where is the joy in life?' you ask. Childcare, housework, working, supporting and loving your husband and family can make you lose track of yourself. You might reason that you need to take Sunday off to have some 'me' time; some peace and quiet whilst your family attend church.

Jesus came to give you a fulfilled life. **The devil wants to rob you of this**. The way he does it is to keep you busy with things that you find boring and unfulfilling which can sap your energy. He tempts you to spend less time with God and then he tempts you to have Sunday as Selfish Sunday. How do I know? I've been there too!!

The devil delights in keeping us away from God.

I have often thought I felt out of it; not part of the church family; that I have worked so hard in the week that I needed to recharge my batteries. God challenged me about this. I realised that church was a time when I built my relationship with God, praised him for all He has done for me and declared what I believe through the worship. When I attended church whilst feeling secretly rebellious about going, God always gave me a word or a special touch. I realised that He blessed me for going, even in the times I went with a **bad** attitude. I had a better Sunday and had energy and strength to face the week ahead.

Heavenly Father,

Thank you for understanding me as no other person can. You never treat me as I deserve and you are loving and encouraging. Enable me to honour you by attending Church. Please enable me to enjoy church and to see the truth that every time I draw near to you, you draw near to me. Help me to get on with other Christians and to resolve any relationship difficulties speedily with your help.

Enable me to have fun with other Christians and always to see them through your eyes and with your love.

If I have to work a Sunday, help me to remember to have a Sabbath remembrance and rest and remember you on another day. I want a relationship with you, my Father God.

Thank you for your loving care and your unconditional love. Amen.

Words to Encourage

Exodus 31 verse 41

"Observe the Sabbath, because it is holy to you."

Leviticus 25 verse 2

"…. The land itself must observe a Sabbath to the Lord."

Deuteronomy 5 verse 12

"Observe the Sabbath day by keeping it holy, as the Lord your God has commanded you."

Isaiah 58 verses 13 and 14.

"If you keep your feet from breaking the Sabbath and from doing as you please on my holy day, if you call the Sabbath a delight and the Lord's holy day honourable, and if you honour it by not going your own way and not doing as you please or speaking idle words, then you will find your joy in the Lord"

17. All That Glitters is not Gold!

An unemployed lady had the bright idea of making a handcart, decorating it with ribbons and bows to make it more attractive to sell things to increase her income. I hadn't a lot of money but thought I really should buy something to encourage her so I peeped into the cart. The stuff was a load of old tatt !! She was obviously selling off her well used belongings. Others might have binned them.

I sometimes think Christianity is like that. We learn our verses, consider our theology and we pluck up courage to ask our friends if they love Jesus. We try to dress it up to look amazing and the answer to all of life's problems. If course, it **IS**. However, I know from experience that it isn't until we *'walk the walk'* in hard times that people really wonder about the reality of our faith.

My Mum and I had many discussions about God. It wasn't until my husband was seriously ill with cancer that she realised I was drawing my strength from God. I was 'walking the walk'. I knew that my husband could die but I trusted God although I found it incredibly tough.

She saw a difference. I'm not saying I always honoured God. I shouted at Him, complained about everything, constantly asked for help but I **did** have a relationship with Him. As it happens, God did miraculously heal my husband. As a result of his illness, he drew closer to God.

When we demonstrate the reality of our faith, for example if our beloved spouse leaves us or we have a bereavement or we lose our jobs or our house floods, then people are drawn to the truth. When we react to bad news do we go under or go to the one who can help? Non Christians in our lives are watching all the time.

Father God,

It says in your word that all things work for good for those who are in Christ Jesus.

I want to be a positive witness for you with the non Christians that I care about. When things go wrong or bad things happen, help me to cast my burdens upon you who will sustain me and carry me through. I want to put my trust in you so that you will consider me a good and faithful servant in the bad times as well as the good ones

Words to Encourage

Proverbs 3 verse 5

"Trust in the Lord your God and lean not on your own understanding; in all your ways acknowledge him and he will make your paths straight."

2 Corinthians   5 verse 20

"We are therefore Christ's ambassadors."

Lamentations 3 verse 22

"Because of the Lord's great love we are not consumed, for his compassions never fail."

St. Francis of Assisi once said:

"Preach the gospel always. If necessary, use words."

18. Fearful or Free

Psalm 34 verse 4

"I sought the Lord and he answered me; he delivered me from all my fears."

When I was little, I had two tortoises. At first, they were frightened of me and, every time they heard my voice or felt me pick them up, they would gasp and retreat into their shells. Soon, when they realised it was me they used to duck their heads out again and let me stroke their wizened necks. I quickly learnt not to hold them on my knee as a milky-green fluid would be we-ed on me!

What am I rambling on about? *We are like tortoises sometimes.* As time goes on and we learn to ask God for more of Him we discover how much He loves each one of us. Deep down, though, we know that there is 'stuff' from our past that needs to be cleared out. Sometimes, we feel challenged to stick our necks out and ask God to sort it; sometimes it is all too much and we retreat into our shells.

A few years ago, I prayed with someone who longed for freedom from the past and from her daily battle with illness. As I finished praying, God gave me a picture of this lady standing in the mouth of a dark tunnel looking out at the light. I told her this and she said it was exactly how she felt. She wanted freedom from her torment but she was afraid to trust God and step **out** of the darkness **into** the light.

We can be standing on a rock and it can give way! We can be in the safety of a dark tunnel and it will fall on us**! The only safe place to be is with God**. Reach out to Him now and ask Him to increase your trust in Him. He knows your fright and will replace it with freedom and peace. He will rescue you.

Lord Jesus,

You came to the earth to be all in all to us; to bring us healing of memories, healing of illness, a new freedom and a life of fulfilment. You sacrificed your life on the cross for me. Give me eyes to see the meaning of the cross and to always remember that the cross is a gesture of love to a world that is hurting. Thank you Jesus.

Or

Lord, I am struggling
with_____

Please give me a wise Christian friend who can pray with me
about_____

Or I am telling you all about this Jesus as I am ashamed and
can't tell anyone

_____

_____

I place this into your hands and ask for healing of this and the
memory _____

Take away my fear of stepping out in faith. Please put in my
path a trustworthy Christian who I can ask for prayer without
even needing to say what it is. Show me if there is anything
further to do but, if not, increase my faith to believe that I can
be set free as the Bible tells me. Amen

19. Your Walk With God and Your Past

Proverbs 14 verse 26

*"He who fears the Lord has a secure fortress, and for his
children it will be a refuge."*

I have a friend who was hurt as a child and has never really got
over it. He said he put his mind to forgetting the past and
moved on but the fact is - he is still tortured by his past and
can't shake free of it. Someone I know will not acknowledge

the past on the assumption that if it is ignored, it is buried and so can't cause pain. I have a friend who constantly bemoans her past and how life is hard.

What's the best way to cope? Setting your mind against the past? Burying the past? Reliving the past?

Only God knows what is best for you. I do firmly believe in the benefits of courses which offer freedom from past issues but, in my case, I also prayed with my prayer partner weekly for some time. I was quite surprised at what the Holy Spirit brought to us both to pray for each other. It was as we prayed that we were set free. We were then both able to go on to serve God in a new way. God couldn't have used me because I was an emotional cripple. I needed to be healed of some past issues so that I could move on and be used and useful to God.

Father God, You know me as no one else does. You know my past and what is happening in my present. Please give me someone godly and trustworthy to pray with about past issues which may be stopping me moving forward as a Christian or being an effective parent.

Or

Father God, I do not want to discuss my past with anyone but I know I can talk to you about *anything*.

I want to tell you
this_____

 I confess and repent
of_____

Holy Spirit, please guide my thinking about anything I need to pray about from my past or present which is holding me down_____

I ask you to help me with my memories of_____

which are affecting my parenthood. I ask that you go back in time and cut me off from_____ in the name of Jesus Christ.

Or.....**Father God,** I'm not sure but I think there may be a barrier in my knowing you as my Father and trusting you the way I want to. Please heal this – I draw near to you God and call out to you to destroy any barriers and help me see you as you are.

Psalm 139 v 23-24   *"Search me, O God, and know my heart; test me and know my anxious thoughts. See of there is any offensive way in me and lead me in the way everlasting."*

20. Anxiety

1 Peter 5 verse 7

"Cast all your anxiety on him because He cares for you."

I have been told that I am super sensitive. This can be a blessing as well as a curse. Being super sensitive can make me super anxious. Being sensitive to the leading of the Holy Spirit is a real blessing that we can all enjoy then we don't need to be anxious! It is something I need to remind myself about. My husband is always optimistic. I have always been a 'what if?'… type of person who prays about what *might* happen as well as what *needs* prayer.

Are you a person who looks on life optimistically or pessimistically? Do you see a glass as half full or half empty? I found that I couldn't change my pessimism but God has done so. The change has been reading the Word of God. I realise that I am the apple of God's eye, *just like you*. I realise that God's beloved Son Jesus Christ died for me so that I might draw near to a Holy God and dare to have a daily relationship with Him and to call Him Father. As I read the Word and see what Jesus did for me personally, I realise that I am *loved and loveable, just like you*. Jesus lived a daily life *just like you and me*. He was brought up in a family. He earned a living. He was the Son of God and yet he had no possessions; He owned no home (Matt.8 v 20 ' *Foxes have holes and birds of the air have nests, but the Son of man has no place to lay his head*.). He had no income when he was in His ministry. He had a life of toil and temptations and mixed with all classes in society. *He understands me and you.* He intercedes for us. **He wants the best for us always**. A believer, a Christian, is someone who is willing to admit imperfection and the need to be more like Jesus. This involves change and challenge but Jesus helps us as we ask Him.

I need to confront any area of weakness or lack of trust in God and confess and repent so that God can change me. Of course I still have a **long** way to go but I am different. *When I have read the Bible and declared it, then there has been a change in my character.* Situations which seem to overwhelm me seem different when I ask the Holy Spirit for His perspective on them. Anxiety seems to be sunk without trace at times like this.

Lord Jesus. Thank you for dying on the cross for me. Thank you for always loving me. Thank you that you understand all about the stresses and strains of daily living and that you will make me more like you if I trust you and ask (pray) for help. I put today's burdens at the foot of your cross and ask you to guide and help me. **Amen**

Panic and Anxiety

"I used to have a handle on life, but it broke!"

(anonymous)

My friend says he isn't happy, but just content. He sorts out his own life in his *own* way. He is in charge and wants **no** advice. I *do* know though that he has black periods.

No one can fully control anxiety or memories which destroy our peace.

I thank my Father God that He hasn't dealt with all the things wrong with me at the same time, or I would have been overwhelmed and despairing if I could see myself the way God does. He is such a loving God and as I call out to Him He never fails to answer me and help me in the way that I need.

John chapter 14 verse 1 *"Do not let your hearts be troubled. Trust in God; trust also in me."*

Are there any practical steps you can take with regard to any recurring anxieties?

- Ask the Holy Spirit 'What is actually causing this anxiety?' Write down what the Holy Spirit tells you. You may think it is one thing but is could actually be something else. Take time with this and keep asking the Holy Spirit to help you. If you feel it's OK to do so, pray with someone else who will never gossip what you say.

- Ask God to enable you to forgive where needed. Remember that forgiveness is **for you**. You are telling God what has happened and asking Him to deal with your hurt and pain. You are then giving Him permission to deal with the situation that hurt you. You need no longer agonize over it. Whenever it comes to your mind again remember that you gave it to God. If necessary keep giving it to God so that the enemy cannot break your peace.

- Unforgiveness can lead to a breakdown in your physical or emotional or mental health. It is actually for your own good that you forgive. Ask God to protect your health and draw near to you. Ask God to show you how much He loves you. No matter what has happened God considers you worthy of His love and faithfulness.

If this is necessary, forgive yourself. Ask God to forgive you and then declare that you accept his forgiveness. Whenever you are tortured by memories just keep giving it all to God until you can truly forgive yourself. God does not want you to live a life crippled by the past!

Words to Encourage

He loves you and will help you always.

James 4 verse 8 *"Come near to God and he will come near to you."*

Ephesians chapter 1, v.18-19 *"I pray also that the eyes of your heart may be enlightened in order that you might know the hope to which he has called you…his incomparably great power for us who believe. "*

21. Trusting God - Friendship with God

Isaiah chapter 2 verse 22 *"Stop trusting in man, who has but a breath in his nostrils. Of what account is he?"*

When a crisis or calamity happens, who do you call on first?

- Your husband

- Your best friend
- Your Mum and Dad
- Your pastor
- God

Someone told me about a man who received the phone call all parents would hate to have. His child was seriously ill in hospital. Instead of diving into his car, he ran upstairs to his bedroom, prostrated himself before God and interceded in prayer for the life of his beloved child. He could have done any one of a dozen things but he recognised the need to call out to his trustworthy God.

A person **can't** rescue in the way God can.   God –

- Hears our prayers 24/7
- Can give back life
- Can work miracles
- Can give us all strength and wisdom to cope
- Loves us unconditionally
- Gives us peace that passes understanding
- Uses *every* circumstance for good

My Father God, I need you to teach me and help me to trust you. Help me to trust in you, confide in you and come to you first. I want to be very close to you God.

Psalm 9 verse 10 *"Those who know your name will trust in you for you, Lord, have never forsaken those who seek you."*

Psalm 37 verses 3-4 *"Trust in the Lord and do good, dwell in the land and enjoy safe pasture. Delight yourself in the Lord and he will give you the desires of your heart."*

Psalm 36 v 5 *"Your love, O Lord, reaches to the heavens, Your faithfulness to the skies."*

Trusting in a faithful God.

Realising He alone has the total picture.

Understanding our helplessness.

Seeking His wisdom.

Thankful He is faithful!

22. Sharper Than Any Double-Edged Sword

Hebrews 4 verse 12.

"For the word of God is living and active. Sharper than any double-edged sword."

Jesus was very straight in what he said about the Bible. In Matthew 5 verses 17-18 He tells us, **'***Do not think that I have come to abolish the Law or the Prophets. I have not come to abolish them but to fulfil them. I tell you the truth, until heaven and earth disappear, not the smallest letter, not the least stroke of a pen, will be any means disappear from the Law until everything is accomplished.***'**

In **John 10 verse 35** Jesus said,*'…Scripture cannot be broken.'*

In **Luke 24 verse 44**…*' Everything must be fulfilled about me that is written about me in the Law of Moses, the Prophets and the Psalms.'*

Some people find it a lot easier to read just the New Testament or even not pick up a Bible – just reading the Bible notes. Trouble is – the notes give us someone's opinion about the scriptures. I am not saying this is wrong but some of the times when God has spoken to me clearly are when I have been reading the Bible by myself, even when I had a bad attitude and didn't want to read the Bible!! **WE NEED THE TOTAL PICTURE,** reading **ALL** of the Bible so we know **ALL** truth.

One day, my family went to church and my mum was harassed as we walked into the packed Harvest Festival service, late. My tiny niece asked loudly, 'what are we here for?'

My mum said, 'SSH, dear! We're here to say thank you to... to... to.... the vicar ....to God...for... all our lovely food.'

The Church, hushed, was suddenly woken up by my niece shouting at the top of her voice, 'THANK YOU VICAR!!'

Circumstances and entrenched thinking can change our interpretation of the Bible. We need to ask God to help us to read and accept the truth in the Bible. Actually it **is** our food.

I was fascinated to read the word *all* here.

2 Timothy chapter 3 verses 16 and 17. *'All Scripture is God-breathed and is useful for teaching, rebuking, correcting and training in righteousness, so that the man of God may be thoroughly equipped for every good work.'*

We're either Christians or we're not. We either read the whole Bible or we don't. God will help all of us if we get stuck or don't understand; we need to ask.

We will then grow in the understanding and love of God and will be rooted and grounded in Him. We will be 'thoroughly equipped for every good work.' Whatever life throws at us we will remember to run to Him knowing we can do nothing but *He can do EVERYTHING.*

We will read the Word, remember the Word; we will be blessed by the Word and we will stand on the Word. I struggled with this too and God helped me!

Father God, Draw us ever closer to you each day. I confess that I have a problem in reading the Bible because_____ I repent and ask for your help. How can I tell people you are amazing unless I see it myself? I know you understand me. I want to read the Bible daily to help me understand you and your ways. I want to read **all** the Bible so that I know **all** of your truth. Amen

"We are all in the gutter, but some of us are looking at the stars."

Oscar Wilde (Irish Poet, Novelist, Dramatist and Critic, 1854-1900)

Answers Given in a Bible Knowledge Test by children

1. The first book of the Bible is Guinness's. In the book of Guinness Adam and Eve were created from an apple (Genesis?).
2. Adam and Eve were created from an apple tree. Noah's wife was Joan of the Ark. Noah built the ark and the animals came on in pears.

3. Moses went to the top of Mount Cyanide to get the 10 Commandments.
4. The first commandment was when Eve told Adam to eat the apple.
5. The seventh commandment is thou shalt not admit adultery.
6. Lot's wife was a pillar of salt by day and a ball of fire by night.
7. Samson slayed the Philistines with the axe of the apostles.
8. The greatest miracle in the bible is when Joshua told his son to stand still and he actually obeyed him.
9. Unleavened bread is bread made with no ingredients.

A Christian should have only one wife
This is called ... monotony.

I don t know the source of this so cannot acknowledge it but it has given me such laughter so I thank whoever wrote this.

23. Feeling Overwhelmed – Relationships

Ephesians 2 verse 14

"For he himself is our peace who has made the two one and has destroyed the barrier, the dividing wall of hostility."

I was praying with my friend about a severed family relationship. In despair, my prayer partner prayed for me,'
Lord, there seems to be no hope. Nothing seems to change, but we know that, even if it seems hopeless, you are a God of power and love. Nothing is too difficult for

you. You are sovereign over this relationship. We declare Jesus came to destroy all the works of the enemy and this relationship can be miraculously healed. We believe you can change everything from bad to good'. She also quoted the above scripture.

Over time, a miraculous change has happened and we do have a relationship where there was none. At times, we have been very close and confided in each other; at times, we have been huffy and apart but we would have *no* relationship *at all* without the miraculous intervention of God. It involves will, forgiveness and God's sovereign power.

If you have difficulty with a relationship ask God for a scripture to declare over the situation, write down what you want to happen and then pray daily.

Lord God

Increase my faith in you. Help me to always be myself but give me wisdom at all times. Heal the wounds and give me a revelation of what you want me to say or do. When I am hurt, help me to forgive and realise I can do nothing but you can do everything. Wrap me in your loving arms and enable me to see this person the way you do. Give me your guidance, your words and your wisdom please Father. Thank you. Amen.

Psalm 25 verse 15 *My eyes are ever on the Lord for only he will release my feet from the snare.*

Psalm 25 verse 3 *"No one whose hope is in you will ever be put to shame.*

Psalm 23 verse 5 *"You prepare a table for me in the presence of my enemies.*

Colossians 3 verse 8 *But now you must rid yourselves of ......anger, rage, malice, slander and filthy language.*

24. Forgiveness

Colossians chapter 3 verses 13-14

"Bear with one another and forgive whatever grievances you may have against each other. Forgive as the Lord forgave you. And over all these virtues put on love, which binds them all together in perfect harmony."

It is not easy to forgive someone who gave you life and then abandoned you; someone who promised to love you always then walked out; someone who was your trusted partner who cheated you out of all your money; someone who didn't let you know of your much-loved brother's illness and subsequent death; someone who bore you children and then ran away with them and you don't know where. It's not easy at all but I know all of these people and they have forgiven those who ripped them apart. They are good people but probably would have found it difficult to forgive without the immense enabling of forgiveness and healing power of God. I know. *I am actually one of those people.*

Are there any tips to get through? Of course not. Every person is different and so every person has to find their own way through the pain. There may be -

a) a period of anger or loss, and

b) a grieving process to get through.

Giving yourself time to cope with shock and loss is important but drawing close to God and expressing how you feel is even more important. I coped by shouting out my pain and then by praising God. It may seem odd but praising God means that you can let go and trust all of the shock, hurt, betrayal and bitterness into His loving hands for healing. It is not easy but God is trustworthy. God understands about forgiveness. He sees us as we are and forgives us and never stops loving us.

Father God, You are the only one who can understand my pain. I confess that I feel_____

I am angry/hurt/bewildered/despairing/worried/ in pain... Please help me to get through this time. I want to tell you about_____and how I feel about_____.

This is what happened and I don't understand this

_____

I want to forgive Father God. Please will you help me to be willing to forgive and to let go of the hurt into your hands. *I don't want to be ill or crippled emotionally as a result of this*. I declare that the past is the past and will not invade my present or future. Your grace helps me to accept what I don't deserve. Help me to remember your grace whenever I am tempted to be unforgiving.

Thank you for your unconditional love for me. Thank you that I am the apple of your eye; that you will never leave me nor forsake me; that I am a loveable person; that I have hope and a future with you.

Help me to see this situation the way you do and leave it all in your hands my loving Father God. You are truly amazing Father. I worship You. **Amen**

25. So What Does the Bible Say About Marriage?

Adam has the answer. The man said,

Genesis 2 v 23-24

'This is now bone of my bone and flesh of my flesh; she shall be called 'woman' because she was taken out of man.

For this reason a man will leave his father and mother and be united to his wife, and they will become one flesh.'

God made Adam but then created a woman as his companion because, **Genesis 2 v 18.** *'It is not good for the man to be alone.'*

This woman, Eve was to be a 'helper' – to be Adam's other half. This does NOT mean that that Eve was inferior to Adam! Reading below we can see there is a <u>**joint**</u> responsibility for the man and woman.

Ephesians 5 verses 22-28

'Wives submit to your husbands as to the Lord, For the husband is the head of the wife as Christ is head of the church, his body, of which he is the Saviour. Now as the church submits to Christ, so also wives should submit to their husbands in everything.. Husbands love your wife just as Christ loved the church and gave himself up for her to make her holy, cleansing her by the washing of water through the word, and to present her to himself as a radiant church, without stain or wrinkle or any other blemish, but holy and blameless. In this same way, husbands ought to love their wives as their own bodies.'

My husband finds headship a tough challenge and says he is not at all comfortable with this. He thinks it likely that many other men struggle with this command especially where they feel unsuccessful with issues of fatherhood. The more we – as couples – work together with God's help – the better the result!

When a Christian man seeks to be a Christian husband and a Christian woman seeks to be a Christian wife there is a balance in their marriage!! Instead of being two selfish beings they are one and this pictures the oneness of Christ with the Church.

Does anyone have the recipe for a happy marriage? Only God. Marriage is God's idea and God's best plan for us because He knows us intimately and knows what we need. It is a lifetime plan, not an interlude ending at a solicitor's with pain and recriminations and bitterness. The plan allows for bad times as well as for good times.

God gets us through the bad times and will help us **when we ask.** Give your burdens to Him who loves you deeply and unconditionally. He knows all about you and your partner and can get you through.

26. Secrets of a Happy Marriage

(the truth is – there are <u>NO</u> secrets for a happy marriage!!)

I made up this poem to illustrate how words can act like battering rams at the security of our marriage. Words can be like weapons. They can maim or poison or kill our marriage. The subject is infidelity but it can be any subject – our pasts, our families, our habits, our hobbies, our friends, our home etc. etc. etc.

Only God knows all about each person and how that person 'ticks' and everything about that person since he or she was born. We can hurt each other easily. Words can trigger past hurts and sensitive areas of our lives.

Especially, we can hurt those we love when tired or anxious or frustrated or angry.

Words are often etched in our memories long after they have been spoken.

Maybe as you read this poem you will see what I mean.

<u>Marriage – Words and their power</u>

<u>(by Annette Baines)</u>

'Nothing can be further from the truth,' she said

As I asked her,' did he, did he sleep in my bed?'

With my rapier tongue

I unravelled the steadfast marriage of ten years.

'Nothing hurts me more than jealousy,' she said

As I asked her, 'did he, did he sleep in my bed?'

And I cannoned words

To mutilate the stalwart marriage of ten years.

'Nothing in the world can make it right now, 'she said

As I cried out, 'did he, did he sleep in my bed?'

And my musket rage

Took lethal aim to kill our marriage of ten years.

'Only God' s hand on us can make it right,' she said

As I cried out,' no, he didn't sleep in my bed!'

And my wreckage shame

Cried out in pain for the killing of ten years' love.

'NO, Nothing can be further from my mind,' she said

As I asked her, 'should I stop sleeping in our bed?'

And she gently kissed

The shame from my face and demonstrated God's grace.

'Nothing is impossible for Lord God,' she said

As I asked her,' why should I sleep with her in bed?'

And she showed her love

As only she could and we fell in love again.

Difficulties, hurts and deep pain need to be expressed but, if you notice the imagery I used, the weapons of anger and spite are lethal and long lasting.

We do fire word guns at our partners from time to time. Asking forgiveness quickly from God and each other **even *if we are in the right*** can take the damage out of our marriage. I have heard of people who have actually **hated** their marriage partners, ***falling in love again*** when all of the hurts and pain and wounds are placed before God and repentance has taken place.

Father God,

I ask that you protect us in times of extreme difficulties or when we are anxious or unhappy. Please let us see each other the way you do and help us to communicate with each other the way you want us to. Help us to pull together as a team to get through problems. **Be with us please God. Amen.**

Ecclesiastes 4 v 12.

"A cord of three strands is not quickly broken."

27. Ouch!

Does it seem as if, no matter what you try in your marriage, you get it wrong?

If you ask too many questions about his day, then you are just nosy. If you forget to ask how the day went then you're not showing any interest in his work.

If he is late back and you tell him you were worried then he says you're fussing, but if you are late back, then he is pacing the floor wondering where you are.

We have to bear with one another in love....and sometimes grit our teeth!

28. A Man's Idea of Helping With the Housework

Ephesians chapter 4 verse 2

"Be completely humble and gentle; be patient, bearing with one another in love."

It's not possible for me to understand what all men are like in the house. Just as every woman is different, so is a man different from another. Just as a man has to bear in love with a wife so a wife is called to bear in love with her husband.

With my own husband, I have found that –

- He doesn't see housework as a pressing need.
- He will do housework but if something more interesting crops up he will postpone it (but to his credit when he remembers he **will complete** what needs to be done).
- When he does a job he does it thoroughly.
- He often doesn't see the detail. He will dust a room but not think about doors or lampshades.
- He loves me to make a list of what needs to be done and then works himself methodically down it. He is conscientious.
- He hasn't a clue what needs to be done on certain days (e.g. changing towels etc).
- When I worked and wanted the house to look nice for the weekend, he might have started a job which plunged the house into chaos. It wasn't what he did; just wrong timing!!

'A spotless house is the sign of a misspent life!'Anonymous

Dear Father God,

You certainly understand my husband and his ways better than I can because you know every detail of his life so far. When I get exasperated or impatient or judgmental about my husband and the way he goes about things then please remind me that you do not treat *me* that way. Give me your love for my husband at all times. Help us to be fair in the distribution of work in the house. Give us both patience and clear channels of communication and trust and love. Amen

Words to Encourage

1 Corinthians 11 verse 3
'Now I want you to realise that the head of every man is Christ and the head of every woman is man, and the head of Christ is God.'

Ecclesiastes 10 verse 4

'....calmness can lay great errors to rest.'

Colossians 3 verses 13 and 14 *Bear with each other and forgive whatever grievances you have against each other. Forgive as the Lord forgave you. And over all these virtues put on love which binds them all together in perfect unity.'*

Ecclesiastes 4 v 12

'..a cord of three strands is not quickly broken. '

29. Married Life – MONEY

*NEWLYWED: The things I cook best are apple pie and steak and kidney pie...

HUSBAND: Which is this?   (anonymous)

'Happy ever after' can seem a dream after a short time of marriage. Suddenly instead of deciding where to party in an evening, you have to decide how to pay the bills and how to sort out your home. Instead of thinking how many holidays you take, you wonder if you can even afford days out.

Some tips given to me...

It's a good idea to write down your money goals – e.g. saving for a dream or holiday or for you to start a family or retirement or moving to a bigger house or making house improvements.

Discuss the right bank accounts. Collect all the information you need. It's simpler to combine pay into a joint account but some couples prefer to have separate accounts.

Have an emergency fund saved up even if it a very small amount you can save. Add to it when you can.

Design your budget. List all your bills then decide how much you can afford to pay for food, petrol etc. Track your budget. One lady I know takes out cash each month and puts them into named tins. She knows to the penny how much she has left for food each month. You could use envelopes instead but remember to keep in a very safe place. Some people put their accounts onto a spreadsheet. This is very useful to give you the total picture.

If you or your partner fail with money remember to treat each other the way God does – no condemnation and finding a way through the problems together. You are a team!

Father God   I need to keep in my memory that every good and perfect gift is from you. Help me in this. Please then guard our finances so that we spend wisely and do not get into debt. Help us to share with each other what we find important in our daily living. Show us how to work as a team and where we need to speak honestly then give us a loving manner and *never* allow us to be condemning. Enable us to trust each other, learning from one another. Enable us to learn from mistakes and discuss ways of improvements with your wisdom and love.

Ecclesiastes 5 verses 10 -11 *'Whoever loves money never has money enough; whoever loves wealth is never satisfied with his income....as goods increase, so do those who consume them. And what benefit are they to the owner except to feast his eyes on them?'*

Luke 16 verse 13 *You cannot serve both God and Money.'*

Ecclesiates 4 v 12*'....a cord of three strands is not quickly broken'*

Proverbs 21 verse 8 *'The way of the guilty is devious, but the conduct of the innocent is upright.'*

Do you spend money and then not tell your husband? Do you feel guilty about the amount you spend on yourself but feel you can't stop? It's far worse to worry about your finances on your own. It can lead to a lot of stress or illness.

Allocate *a regular money date* when you come together and think about how to spend your money for the benefit of both of you. If you feel that your husband has any problems with money, you might point out that organising your finances gives you peace of mind. If he still refuses to discuss finances, then you might make up a budget for him to look at. As a very final resort, you could do as a friend did. Her husband was unemployed, drifted into drugs and got into debt with drug dealers. They paid off the dealers, moved house and her husband took the first job he could. She kept tight control of finances and cut up all the credit cards. Fifteen years on, they are happily married. I don't ask if the arrangements have changed. It's none of my business. However, if you feel that you are drifting into debt because of gambling, drugs etc. then take advice right away. It is serious and can rip your marriage and family apart. Organisations like CAP (CHRISTIANS AGAINST POVERTY) and Citizen's Advice can support you. There is always hope.

Father God,

I ask that you help us with our finances. As husband and wife, we are 'one' in your eyes and so should never keep secrets from each other. Enable us to trust each other and to be accountable to each other in a loving and helpful way. If we need to budget, show us how to do so. If we need to make changes to our lifestyle, help us to do so. If we cannot agree, show us where to go for help and mediation. Please do not allow us to dishonour you in our finances. Please give us disquiet in our spirits when we are tempted to be deceitful. If we are unwise then prompt us to confess it to each other and to you God. Help us to remember that success can come out of failure. Amen.

Nothing is worse than doing nothing.

Ask God what to do.

List all of your debts and then list all of your income. There are good budget sheets on the internet. Pray and take advice (e.g. CAP).

<u>There is nothing that can't be solved with God</u>.

Matthew 6 verse 24 *"No one can serve two masters. Either he will hate the one and love the other, or he will be devoted to the one and despise the other. You cannot serve both God and Money."*

Francis Bacon 1561-1626 British Philosopher

Prosperity is not without many fears and disasters and adversity is not without comforts and hopes.

Finances

1. Share money management. Both should take part in making decisions about how much to spend and what to spend it on. Be honest and open at all times. It's not worth trying to conceal anything; many couples have found this out! It's also not worth being mistrusting. You are married. You are a couple. Talk and never conceal anything. Discuss what really matters to you. For example haircuts might be bottom of a husband's list but top of a wife's list!! It's OK to say what means a lot to you, so you can make sure that you are both happy as a couple. You could jointly make a 'wish list' and work out together how your wishes could be achieved. You might consider a special treat and how it might be budgeted for.

2. Write down all of your income and expenditure (budget form from e.g. CAP or internet) Make sure you include any standing orders. Some only occur each quarter and so you could be fooled into thinking you have more money in hand than you thought. Also roughly estimate how much you will be spending on gifts, postage etc. This will show you how much money you have left and are able to save.

3. Track your budget each month. Look ahead to the next months so that if you have heavy bills arriving you will not be dismayed.

4. If you are thinking of investments as a form of saving, agree as a couple the level of risk you are both prepared to take. Listen carefully to each other.

5. Think of yourself as a perfect team. There may be tricky times and tricky subjects but remember you are a team and so will always pull together to resolve any difficulties. Encourage each other. Use each other's strengths and make sure you make allowances for each other's weaknesses. If you mess up, say so. Remember you BOTH have weaknesses.

6. Be determined to speak to each other in love. If heated arguments occur, have 'timeout' with a cup of tea or a walk to calm down.

7. Don't make accusations – stick to the facts if your spouse is overspending. If you have made mistakes in spending, be honest. State the facts – that overspending has occurred and ask your spouse what you can do to put it right. Make sure that he will do the same.

8. Learn from each other. Have weekly money meetings so that you both know where you are financially. This takes a lot of strain off the marriage! This will help you to communicate better and build more openness and understanding.

9. Build an emergency fund. This is separate from your holiday fund! This is for emergencies only! When there is sudden illness, lost job, major home repairs or any other disaster you will be able to cope.

10. Save for retirement.

11. Remember – marriage comes down to the vows you made. Money troubles are not a good reason to walk out. You can

use this time to build real lasting intimacy and trust with your spouse.

12. Be determined to be debt free. If you get into debt, take professional advice. Never take out loans to pay off your debt. Fix a budget with a professional and reliable agency like CAP and set your mind on a two month goal of payment, then another two month goal rather than look at the total and feel helpless. Consider your repayments for debt a priority but don't worry about them. You will be amazed at how quickly you can be debt free. At CAP office, they cheer and praise God every time someone becomes debt free!

God can help us do anything.

30. Divorce

Malachi 2 verses 13-16

"Another thing you do: You flood the Lord's altar with tears. You weep and wail because he no longer pays attention to your offerings or accepts them with pleasure from your hands. You ask, 'why?' It is because the Lord is acting as the witness between you and the wife of your youth, because you have broken faith with her, although she is your partner, the wife of your marriage covenant.

Has not the Lord made them one? In flesh and spirit they are his. And why one? Because he was seeking godly offspring. So guard yourself in your spirit, and do not break faith with the wife of your youth. 'I hate divorce', says the Lord God of Israel."

As I understand it, 'faith' in someone seems to be identical to loyalty. How loyal are you to your husband? Are you ever negative about him? Do you discuss his irritating habits or shortcomings with trusted friends? I ask these questions knowing that I failed in this respect.

My husband is the love of my life but I've only just realised the power of the negative words I have spoken about him. I believe that even though my marriage has been blessed, that it would have been better had I only spoken to God. Actually, critical words are abusive. Many people looked at our marriage and declared that we had nothing in common. I often accepted that attitude. My husband refused to accept it and declared that we share our faith and also the same outlook on life. My husband runs his own Outdoor Pursuits business whilst I am more passive. We are opposites but complement each other perfectly and love spending time together. Interestingly, the ones who criticised our marriage and had partners who shared the same interests are not now together!!

We need to speak out the positives in our marriage. There will always be gorgeous/sexy/intelligent/fun people who come into our lives from time to time but they can never meet our needs the way our loving husbands can. Comparisons and daydreams lead to negativity then divorce. Instead, *pray changes* into your marriage.

Father,

When I am exasperated, irritated, tired or anxious about my relationship with my husband, please bring to my mind the positives. Each day, give us a fresh understanding of each other and a desire to affirm and love each other. Enable us to bear with one another in love, especially at crisis times when it is so easy to look on the black side of things. If we want our jobs, our homes, our children to be blessed, then we need to repent of any negativity towards our husbands. You witness all we do and say. Help us to change if needed and to have faith that **we** cannot change our husband but **you** can Father God.

31. Torn Apart

Malachi 2 verses 13 – 16

'Another thing you do: You flood the Lord's altar with tears...

Has the Lord not made them one? In flesh and spirit they are His. And why one? Because He was seeking godly offspring. So guard yourself in your spirit, and do not break faith with the wife of your youth. 'I hate divorce', says the Lord God of Israel.'

I haven't divorced but I have seen my friends go through the agony of rejection, pain, despair and bewilderment. Naturally, I have no answers. There have been many problems, difficulties and stresses in my marriage but we have been so blessed by the right people being in place at the right time to pray for us and then to give advice.

If you are reading this and contemplating leaving, then I would say to you something I have observed. Once you leave, it can be 10 times more difficult to return.

If your husband hasn't met your needs and you have found someone else, I would say to you that I have observed that the problems from the first marriage eventually re-surface in the second marriage once the 'honeymoon' period is over.

If you think that you have strong, resilient children who can cope with your divorce, then I can tell you of many children I have seen whilst teaching whose learning has been arrested by a deep pain that they haven't got the words to articulate. They often feel it's their fault. They have such a sense of loss that it can affect them all of their lives. I spent a lot of time with a school secretary who was devastated at the divorce of her parents when they retired. She was AN ADULT but couldn't cope! I am NOT saying children *can't* cope but from my experience *can* say it has an effect on them. Isn't it better for them not to <u>have to</u> cope?

If you think that your husband won't miss or be affected by your going, remember that you promised God to be faithful to each other and so became one. It will be a wrench for everyone concerned because it is not God's best plan.

You have to decide what's best for you. Someone told me she so wished she had given herself TIME. She didn't give her marriage time to be sorted. She left her husband, felt lonely and then met a man who was kind. She married him and quickly realised she had made a big mistake. She could see that her first marriage would have worked *with time*.

Dear Father God, See what I am going through! Wrap your loving arms around me and help me see what is best   Please can you give me the right people to help (who will not betray my confidences) and maybe even a good Christian counsellor so we can resolve difficulties.

Give me wisdom and trust in you to stay and make changes so that I can always say to my children that I didn't give up too easily and I tried to do what I could do.

Do I stay or do I go? Guide my thinking God. Help me through this.

Whatever happens, I know that you will always love me, Father God.

32. Temptation - God's Power is Greater!

Hebrews 10 v 18

"Because He himself suffered when He was tempted, He is able to help those who are being tempted."

The soft dagger-whisper in the ear of Eve when tempted by the enemy Satan; the voice of a 'friend' telling you you're a wuss if you don't at least try drugs once; the promise of a thrilling win as you gamble; the voice that whispers that no one loves you so you may as well die; the boyfriend who promises eternal faithfulness if only you sleep with him; your friends who encourage you to go out and drink yourself silly; the work colleague who shows you with his eyes that you are attractive to him, and praises your work; that inner voice that whispers that you are unlovable and so you may as well eat and drink your fill to comfort yourself; the friend's husband who is **so** easy to get on with; that new outfit that beckons you and begs to be stolen. These are the seductive voices of a fallen angel called Satan or the devil or the enemy. Temptations are used by the enemy to destroy us.

How do we avoid this? The enemy usually attacks us when we are most vulnerable – when we have had little sleep; when we have had a row with our husband; when we have money/sex or other problems. When people have told me how things have happened it is obvious that the enemy has exploited their weaknesses at a time when they are feeling low or 'down' because of circumstances. How can you sort this? First of all, confess your temptation and anything you did to God; ask His forgiveness and ask Him to give you determination not to sin in this way again. *Surrender* this area of weakness to Him. **READ** the Bible promises and find an appropriate scripture and declare it daily. For example Philippians 4 v 13, *'I can do everything through Him who gives me strength.'* The enemy is then immobilised. If someone hurt you and that hurt led you to sin then **surrender your hurt** to God and ask Him to enable you to forgive. If needed pray with a trustworthy and wise Christian friend and be accountable to her if you still struggle with this. Ring her whenever you're tempted. A voice of caution – bitter church experiences proved that one is advisable to never confide in a male friend or Christian friend. Male friends comforting females has sometimes led to a lot of unnecessary pain and trauma for all concerned.

Ask God who to talk to.

Father God,

I confess I am being tempted in the area of.. Please enable me to forgive myself. I understand that being tempted is not a sin because even Jesus was tempted, but I ask that you provide a way out of this temptation.

I ask that you show me a scripture I can declare out loud to strengthen my resolve against temptation.

I surrender my temptation and my circumstances into your hands and I thank you that I am not alone - you are in this with me.

Please guide my thinking as to what to do and say and please don't let my mind be anguished about this.

Please give me healthy and happy occupations to ease the tension in my mind and body. Amen

33. Temptation - The Grass is Always Greener!

Hebrews 10 verse 8

"Because he himself suffered when he was tempted, he is able to help those who are being tempted."

Isn't it amazing that Jesus Christ, the Son of God, faced temptations just as we face temptations today? It says in the Bible that Jesus is the *'radiance of the Father's glory and the exact representation of His being'*, (Hebrews 1 verse 3). Jesus described Himself – '*anyone who has seen me has seen the Father*', (John 14 verse 9).

Pause for a moment and meditate on these scriptures.

Jesus, Holy, the Son of God was tempted just as we are tempted. *HOLY, tempted*.

If we look at the accounts in Matthew and Luke (chapters 4) we can see **why and how** Jesus overcame temptation. Jesus mentioned the devil and warned us of the devil many times. Jesus was himself tempted and it was **not** easy for Him.

Satan's plans were to exploit Jesus at a weak time when He had had no food for five weeks and five days. He tried to distract Him from His mission, enticing Him to use His power for himself, distorted scripture to attempt to cause Him to sin and then tempted Him to seize political power and popularity by performing a miracle to glorify himself.

How could Jesus combat the devil? He is the Son of God. However, it started when he was a boy. He had godly parents. As a Jewish son, He was taught all the scriptures in the Old Testament. He knew them. He must have heard them all more than once. He must have learnt them and absorbed them. He used the scriptures to invalidate the devil's arguments. He knew His Father God and knew that He could never use His own power for himself (in the Bible, when Jesus performed miracles it was for the good of others - *never* to meet His own needs). It must have been tempting to turn stones into bread as He could readily do, but He resisted this temptation. He resisted the temptation to seize political power. This would have earned him support from His fellow Jews as 'a political messiah' and Jesus would **not** have to face the daunting prospect of the cross. The jumping from the Temple would have had the people in awe and prove that He was the messiah. Jesus resisted the devil as we can do. *He showed us the way to resist the devil.*

Our temptations can be put into these categories: bodily needs, power (control) and attempts to be popular. Satan is still using these tactics and times them to be when we are tired, unhappy, sick or busy. We can choose to immediately call to God for help or instead of seeking God, we suffer our sin.

I Corinthians 10 v 13 *'no temptation has seized you except what is common to man. And God is faithful; He will not let you* *be tempted beyond what you can bear. But, when you are tempted, He will also provide a way out so that you can stand under it.'*

Father God, help me to remember that it is not sinful to be tempted. We are all tempted; even Jesus was tempted. *When* I am tempted, help me to declare the truth that you will provide a way out of this temptation. Even if I feel weak, remind me to draw near to you for your protection and help.

Thank you that you hear every prayer Father!! Amen.

34. One Man's Food is Another Man's Poison!

Pickled ram's testicles and rotting shark meat are Icelandic delicacies. In Australia, aboriginals eat chopped kangaroo tails and sugar ants whilst fresh snake meat is available in Hong Kong. What about your food?

What do you do when your marriage partner is vegetarian and you are not? When you have a stomach problem and can't eat out? When you are Coeliac and he is not? When your footie husband will only eat junk food? When you hate anyone watching you eating and your husband loves entertaining and eating out? When your husband's favourite foods are highly spiced and you can't tolerate them? When your husband and children have allergies?

One man's food can be another man's poison. Basically, all you can do is agree to adapt or compromise and try to keep everything *simple*. This is true when your views clash on finance, bringing up the children, visits to your in-laws, friendships, holidays, doing the housework and DIY, his work, your work, his hobbies, your hobbies. The devil loves married couples to fight. Be determined to resolve conflict God's way.

You might list the things that are bothering you. Highlight the really important ones. Pray about how to discuss the subject and **time it** for when your partner isn't tired, you have the time, there is no important football game on TV and no distractions!

If you feel that you are not being listened to then use the 'broken record' approach. Keep sticking to the facts and make your point over and over.

If you are still not listened to, ask a wise Christian friend to pray with you. There may be blockages to listening. One husband refused to discuss any areas of conflict with his wife because he had a grandma who was a dictator and he was determined inwardly that he would only do what **he** wanted to do and *no one* would tell **him** what to do. It wasn't until his wife was leaving him that he realised that he should have treated her respectfully. Thankfully she prayed about it, gave him another chance and they have been married for over 30 years!

Colossians 3 verse 13 and 14 *'Bear with one another and forgive whatever grievances you may have against one another. Forgive, as the Lord forgave you. And over all these virtues put on love, which binds them all together in perfect unity.'*

Father God, nothing is impossible for you. Help us to communicate!! We need you to highlight how to problem solve. Please show us God. Amen

Words to Encourage

Ecclesiastes 4 v 12

'...A cord of three strands is not quickly broken.'

35. Pornography

Romans 12 verse 2 *"Do not conform any longer to the pattern of this world, but be transformed by the renewing of your mind."*

It was late one night. My husband was at a meeting and I flicked channels. I was absolutely astounded and aghast at what I saw and I could not turn off the TV. I actually couldn't believe my eyes. It was so shocking and bizarre.

My friend says I am a natural prude. However, only God, my husband and I know that I am not really a prude. That image was so powerful that I couldn't shake it out of my head and my spirit. I had to call out to God quite a few times before the power of the image over my mind died.

I have been told that pornography is addictive and I can quite believe it. People say that there are different levels and some of it is harmless but I disagree.

We don't have to act as prudes but we can stand for what is right. It is a fact the marriage bed is meant to be pure and loving where we meet our husband's sexual needs and he meets ours. If we have difficulties then we can call out to God. He invented sexual intercourse and he has answered the prayers of many Christians in this area of their marriage. I know that sounds too simple and good to be true but it is a fact that as James says in chapter 3 verses 7-10, '**Submit you, then, to God. Resist the devil and he will flee from you. Come near to God and he will come near to you. Wash your hands, you sinners, and purify your hearts,   Humble yourselves before the Lord and he will lift you up.'**

Father God,   pornography can make a person double-minded and can eventually destroy a marriage, peace of mind and self-respect. Help us to see pornographic images the way you do.

Help us to cleanse ourselves by turning to you and confessing sin whenever tempted. Enable us to have a loving, mutually satisfying, sexual relationship with our husband. There is no condemnation for those who are in Christ Jesus so help us to communicate any problems or difficulties in a loving and caring way to each other and to you.

Answer the desire of our hearts to have a marriage that is deeply caring and loving all the days of our lives.

Father God help us in the area
of_____
and let us rest in the knowledge that you **will** help us as you want us to have a long and happy marriage. Enable us to forgive ourselves if needed and to walk free of torturing thoughts. Thank you God. Amen.

Words to Encourage

Romans 8 verse 6-7.

'The mind of sinful man is death, but the mind controlled by the spirit is life and peace, the sinful mind is hostile to God. It does not submit to God's law nor can it do Those controlled by the sinful nature cannot please God.'

36. Computer Games

Proverbs 4 verses 26 and 27 *"Make level paths for your feet And take only ways that are firm. Do not swerve to the right or the left;   Keep your foot from evil."*

I felt nauseated and revolted when a visiting non-Christian friend answered his mobile. He was discussing a boxing computer game with a friend and described with glee how the graphics showed his 'punches' and the 'smashed face and blood' of his computer game opponent.

This young man had been physically abused as a child and I realised that the game served as an anger outlet.

Should Christians play computer games? My answer would be ask God. Pray. Be prepared to be obedient if God says 'no' and don't be surprised if he says 'yes'. I would say this though. Every time you watch a violent or wicked act, even if you just think it is a bit of fun, it has an effect on your spirit and your walk with the Lord. You can become desensitised to goodness.

What happens if you accidentally watch pornography or a violent or occult image?

Run to God. Ask for his forgiveness and for Him to cleanse you and take the image away. God already knows what you did.

 Proverbs 5 verse 21 *'For a man's ways are in full view of the Lord, and he examines all his paths.'*

Only God can heal you from the effects of impure images or acts of abuse. He always has a rescue package which can transform every life and take away the darkness.

Dear Lord and Father of all mankind, You know we are often weak. Forgive our foolishness where we have been unwise; forgive our weakness where we have knowingly done something which is ungodly. Please cleanse our hearts from all unclean images. Please enable us to release all of the violent, unclean or wicked images of the past and present them to you in prayer so that they no longer have a hold over us. We repent of doing anything which is wrong in your sight. If we need further to pray, give us wise Christian friends to share with who will never gossip away our past to others.

Guard our spirits, hearts and minds in future Lord. You are a strong tower – when we are tempted let us run to you and call for help. Remind us that when we do the right thing you always bless us for obedience.

Words to Encourage

Hebrews 10 verse 22   *"Let us draw near to God with a sincere heart in full assurance of faith, having our hearts sprinkled to cleanse us from a guilty conscience."*

Psalm 72 verse 13 **"**He will take pity on the weak"...

37. What is a Friend?

I was thinking about how much I value my close friends. They are set apart from other friends because of the passage of time and the development of trust. However, I have learnt also to listen to the Holy Spirit. I just met someone and felt that God showed me that this person is lovely – trustworthy - and would be a good friend.

So what does make a good friend?

- Someone you can connect with (for me, mainly as a Christian but also as a friend).
- Someone you can share ideas or interests with.

- Someone who is fun.
- Someone who isn't demanding or domineering.
- Someone who will NEVER gossip about you.
- Someone who can offer good advice or find information or help you in any way.
- Someone who can identify my gifts, talents or abilities and encourage me to use them for God (and whom I can encourage as I identify hers/his).
- Someone who will give me the right level of support and encouragement, accepting me as I am and putting me straight in an affirming way if I am in the wrong.
- Someone who can strengthen my faith in God.
- Someone who doesn't manipulate me into doing what she wants but who is honest and able to speak to me frankly.

You might think differently. Also, I have found that I can have a laugh with people I have nothing in common with; no shared faith or interests.

- Do you find it easy to make friends or are you a loner?
- Do you find social occasions a torture or a joy?

    Be assured that God knows all that you go through.
    Talk to God. He can help you.

Father God, I confess before you that I find other people_____

I confess that I find it hard to make friendships as I am shy or

_____

I confess that I find it easy to make friends but I cannot keep my friendships. Please show me what a good friend is and help me to be a good friend.

93

I confess that because of ....I find it difficult to trust friends. Help me to have wisdom in what I share and help me to have good friendships in the future.

I confess Father that I do not trust friends because they have hurt/betrayed/been judgemental/gossiped about me. Please help me to forgive them the way that you forgive me. Show me who I can open up to in future and please heal the distrust I feel. Help me to see all Christians and friends the way you do, with your wisdom and love and acceptance.

Words to Encourage

Proverbs 18 verse 24 *"A man of many companions may come to ruin, but there is a friend who sticks closer than a brother."*

38. Friendship

When friends hurt us, retaliation is often on our minds. God would have us forgive. Maybe, though, before we forgive, it's worth talking it through with our friends in order to make sense of what has happened, and find out WHY they hurt us. Sometimes, it's best to leave well alone and not discuss anything. As you pray, God will guide you in the right thing to do.

When I've been upset by friends, I've felt like not seeing them again. This is just what the devil wants. I do feel it's worth fighting for friendships and 'bearing with one another in love.' (Ephesians 4 v 2) Is there a case for letting people go though?

I reckon that if friends pull you down then 'yes'. I would always pray and take advice from God first however.

I have had friends for a number of years and they upset me from time to time but I know them well and it's usually when they are under pressure that they're thoughtless. Often, they confide things and I can see their underlying anxieties. They don't directly speak out what's on their minds. I have had friends with health problems who have assured us all that they are fine. They LOOK fine but if you know them well, you see their worry. Familiarity doesn't breed contempt; it builds understanding, a bond of affection and a sense of family. *Spending time with friends is wonderful for all concerned because it is a network of support and affirmation and trust.*

Father God

You see myself and my friend. If I am hurt, I need you to remind me to forgive my friend the way that you always forgive me. Give me eyes to see my friend the way you do; ears to hear and understand the way you do; hands to support and encourage the way you do.

Above all, don't let my friendship die unless this relationship is bad for me. Amen

Ephesians 4 verse 2

"Be completely humble and gentle; be patient, bearing with one another in love."

Dear friend – did you know..

'Fashion is a form of ugliness so intolerable that we have to alter it every six months...'

Oscar Wilde 1854 -1900. Anglo Irish novelist, playwright and poet.

'We've got to go out on a limb sometimes because that's where the fruit is.

Will Rogers 1879 – 1935. American actor and humourist.

We appreciate frankness from those who like us. Frankness from others is called insolence. Andre Maurois 1885 – 1967. French biographer, novelist and essayist.

'You can't put off being young until after you retire.'

Philip Larkin 1922 -1985. British poet and novelist.

'You can't build a reputation on what you are GOING to do.'
Henry Ford 1863 – 1947. American automobile industrialist.

39. The Best of Friends!

Psalm 1, verse 1

'Blessed is the man who does not walk in the counsel of the wicked or stand in the way of sinners or sit in the seat of mockers.'

The people you, your spouse and your children hang out with will shape your future and influence your present. <u>A friend can affirm you, encourage your faith, support you or cheer you. Or a friend can tease you mercilessly (leading to self-doubt), gossip or be negative about your circumstances (leading to discouragement), be too impatient, busy or distracted to help you (leading to depression and insecurity) and can be a voice of doom when you need a good laugh.</u>

Psalm 1 warns us about our friendships. A person who has mainly non-Christian friends will absorb their life thoughts. He or she will be used to their teasing remarks but where is the boundary line? What do you do when people you like mock or deny the existence of God and Jesus? What do you do when they give you worldly advice which contradicts Christian teaching? Psalm 1 shows us the benefits of living a good life, *'whatever he does prospers'*. **God never fails to bless us for right living**. Verse 6, ' *For the Lord watches over the way of the righteous, but the way of the wicked will perish.'*

Lord God,

I don't want to lose my friends but please help me to see them the way that you do. Please don't let me put my friends on a pedestal. Bring godly friends into my life and show me how to be a good friend. Open my eyes to see people the way you do. Prompt me to run to you first with any troubles.

You are my true friend who can rescue, help, encourage, support, protect, nurture and always be there for me. Only you can truly help me with my life problems. Let my children see my trust in you. **Amen**

Words to Encourage

Proverbs 13 verse 20 *'He who walks with the wise grows wise, but a companion of fools suffers harm.'*

Proverbs 2 verse 12 *'Wisdom will save you from the ways of wicked men, from men whose words are perverse, who leave the straight paths to walk in dark ways who delight in doing wrong and rejoice in the perverseness of evil, whose paths are crooked and who are devious in their ways.'*

Psalm 40 verse 8 *'I desire to do your will, O my God; your law is within my heart.'*

Psalm 34 verse 4 *'I sought the Lord and he answered me; he delivered me from all my fears.'*

40. Gossip

'Whispers are like daggers. They stab you between the shoulder blades when you are not looking.'

From ' Secret Sins' by Katherine Haig

Gossips can –

- Cause feelings of betrayal
- Smash self-esteem
- Break friendships forever

When a family had problems, their church was amazingly supportive and helpful. Praying, helping financially, giving child support, encouraging and helping. The couple involved were quite O.K. with all of the details of their lives being made public and thankful for help.

Another family had problems. The parents were very quiet, private individuals. They asked confidentially for prayer but the church took over and made arbitrary decisions for the family. The couple loathed their problems being aired in public and felt unloved, judged and angry for people's judgemental attitude towards them. The Church thought they did the right thing but it reinforced feelings of failure and family problems for many years and is still not resolved. Church members' gossip about the situation was obvious so they moved to another church, but it took a long time before they were able to trust again. People in that church did not know the harm they were doing because they just made decisions without asking God.

I was a gossip before I was a Christian. I always reasoned that I needed to know what was happening so I didn't put my foot in it. I was never a malicious gossip but what I did was wrong.

It is true that **'the tongue has the power of life and death'** (Proverbs 18 verse 21). Even if you are concerned about a friend *never* tell anyone else what it is about even if your only desire is to get her the help she needs. If your friend finds out you gossiped she will never trust you again. It is up to *your friend* to ask others for help or prayer, *not you*. You can pray for her though and God will intervene when you do so. God will always meet her needs when you pray. He knows her better than you or anyone else.

Prayer is the most powerful and loving thing you can do for a friend.

Father God – Psalm 139 tells us that you see everything that happens to us. Also that, 'before a word is on my tongue you know it completely O Lord.' (verse 4). When I am tempted to betray a friend by gossiping, even with good intentions, please put a Holy Spirit check on me so that I do not step outside of your will for me.

Help me to pray faithfully for my friend knowing that you are the only person who can fully help her.

Proverbs 11 verse 13

'A gossip betrays a confidence, but a trustworthy man keeps a secret.'

Daniel 10 verse 12

....Since the first day that you set your mind to gain understanding and to humble yourself before your God, your words were heard ....

Only God knows what your friend needs. Your prayers are powerful and God hears EVERY WORD from the first word of the first time you pray.

Seeds of Growth and Love

March 2015 .....God showed me about the church. He loves us all.

There are Church members who are like flowers tight in bud. They have the potential to be the most beautiful scent, colour or shape but they keep tight shut. They are upright - having grown up and *are* strong but they do not open up!

Being camouflaged in the congregation is safer and neutral. It's safer to stay tight closed rather than to be ourselves.

God created us to burst forth in beautiful shapes, colours and textures – all different! Are you like me and find it difficult to just be yourself in a Church situation?

I am praying for myself and for you that God will enable us to relax and to be ourselves at Church. Perhaps you would like to join me?

Father God,

You know why I find it difficult to be at Church. Thank you that you bless me every time I attend and you know everything about me.

Please enable me to relax and be myself at church. Please enable me to remember your approval and love of me.

Please enable me to continue to be faithful in prayer for all of the church members and please enable all of the church to see each other the way you do.

Please open my eyes to see my attendance at church the way you do. If you wish me to serve in any way other than by prayer then open the doors so that I can see your will for me. If not please close all doors.

Thank you for your love and faithfulness towards me.

Open my eyes to see myself the way you do. Help me to JUST BE MYSELF, THE WAY YOU CREATED ME TO BE.

I love you Father God.

41. Seeds of Growth and Love in your Family

When you plant seeds have you ever looked closely at them in your hand? They are mostly different in size, shape and colour. They will grow differently and will need different conditions (temperature, soil, light, water) in order to flourish and grow strong. **These seeds are like you and your family**. They have the potential to be seedlings then to bud and then to flower or fruit. These are the stages of a person's growth.

Just as the growth of plants can be affected by winds, rain, frost damage and neglect so your family '*seeds*' can also fail to thrive. If illness or difficulties or pain or disappointments or anguish or attack or hurts or damage by others occurs to these lovely people then like seeds growth can be arrested.

Instead of that beautiful flower there can be stunted growth, and buds tightly shut where they should be open to show the flower's inner beauty. Going away from God and leading an imperfect, even damaged, life can follow. Even worse - people can *attend* Church but are *closed off* to God so *can't* receive God's blessings.

Family life can be like a roller coaster. Just when you think your life with your husband and children is going on OK then life seems to fall apart. There will always be problems but you are *never* alone.

Jesus is the one who is always there for you. He tells us in **Matthew 11 verses 28-29,**

'Come to me, all you who are weary and burdened and I will give you rest. Take my yoke upon you and learn from me , for I am gentle and humble in heart, and you will find rest for your souls. For my yoke is easy and my burden is light..'

You are priceless!

As a wife and mother your prayers are the glue that holds your family together. Your daily walk with God and surrendering your marriage, family concerns, problems and futures to Him will bless you and bless your marriage and your parenthood.

God loves you all deeply and the many promises in His word show us that He is a loving, nurturing Father to us all.

Praying daily for your children's relationship with God and for their wellbeing will help to take them out of the bud stage into the flowering stage.

Reading the Word will have a powerful impact on your family.

Sharing your faith is a powerful witness to your precious children.

Nothing you can do for them will have greater value than encouraging their relationships with God.

God bless you all!!